Christmas 2004

The Tall Firs

The Story of the University of Oregon & The First NCAA Basketball Championship

Joe R. Blakely

Also by Joe R. Blakely

THE BELLFOUNTAIN GIANT KILLERS

THE STORY OF A SMALL OREGON HIGH SCHOOL AND ITS MIRACULOUS CHAMPIONSHIP SEASON

Photo courtesy University of Oregon Athletic Media Services

Celebrating the University of Oregon's NCAA basketball championship, 1939

In 1939, the University of Oregon roused the Pacific Northwest from the hardships of the Great Depression as its basketball team, known as the "Tall Firs," achieved fame on a national stage and elevated the sport to new levels of popularity. This is a story of that team.

THE TALL FIRS

HISTORICAL PHOTOGRAPHS PROVIDED THROUGH THE COURTESY OF
University of Oregon Athletic Media Services
University of Oregon Knight Library
Mr. and Mrs. Ford Mullen

PUBLISHED BY
Bear Creek Press
814 Couch Avenue • Wallowa, Oregon 97885
541-886-9020 • bearcreekpress@eoni.com
www.bearcreekpress.com

PRINTING HISTORY
Bear Creek Press First Edition, March 2004

Printed in the United States of America.

ISBN: 1-930111-40-1

Bear Creek Press

World Headquarters located in Wallowa, Oregon U.S.A.
(at the old Abbie Riggle place on Bear Creek Road).

I wish to dedicate this book to my brother and sister-in-law,
Larry and Ruth Blakely.

Photo courtesy University of Oregon Athletic Media Services

ACKNOWLEDGMENTS

In writing this book, I found several written sources to be invaluable, especially Howard Hobson's *Shooting Ducks*, Jeff Eberhart's "Q & A With Ret. Rear Adm. John Dick" in *Oregon Quarterly* (Summer 2003), and *The Oregonian* newspaper of the period.

In addition, L.H. Gregory, *The Oregonian's* sports writer of the day, captured the excitement of basketball with class, with passion, and with humor. He not only provided in-depth coverage of the games themselves, but also a wealth of information about what was happening on the sidelines—and he could usually coax a frequent grin or an occasional tear from readers. He coined the nickname "Tall Firs" and followed them from their sophomore year to their final championship.

Of the three surviving Tall Firs—John Dick, Robert Hardy, and Ford Mullen—I was able to interview Mr. Hardy and Mr. Mullen, and I thank them for their time as well as for their stories of those championship days.

I also wish to thank the University of Oregon Knight Library, especially the Microfilm Records Department, the Special Collections (Archives) Department, and the Map Department. Other libraries consulted were the Eugene Public Library, the Oregon State Library in Salem, and the Washington State Library in Olympia.

Other people to whom I am grateful include Saundra Miles, Dan Williams, Kenny King, Albert Erickson, Glen Hebert, Kirk Johansen, Beverly Dawson, Becky Snieder, Vivian Wheeler, Scott McNeeley, William E. Love, John Bryant, Don Hunter, Francis Warren, Sue Miller, Lee Temple, and Greg Walker of the University of Oregon Athletic Media Services Office.

Lastly, let there be no mistake about this: I am a writer by virtue of my publisher, Mark Highberger.

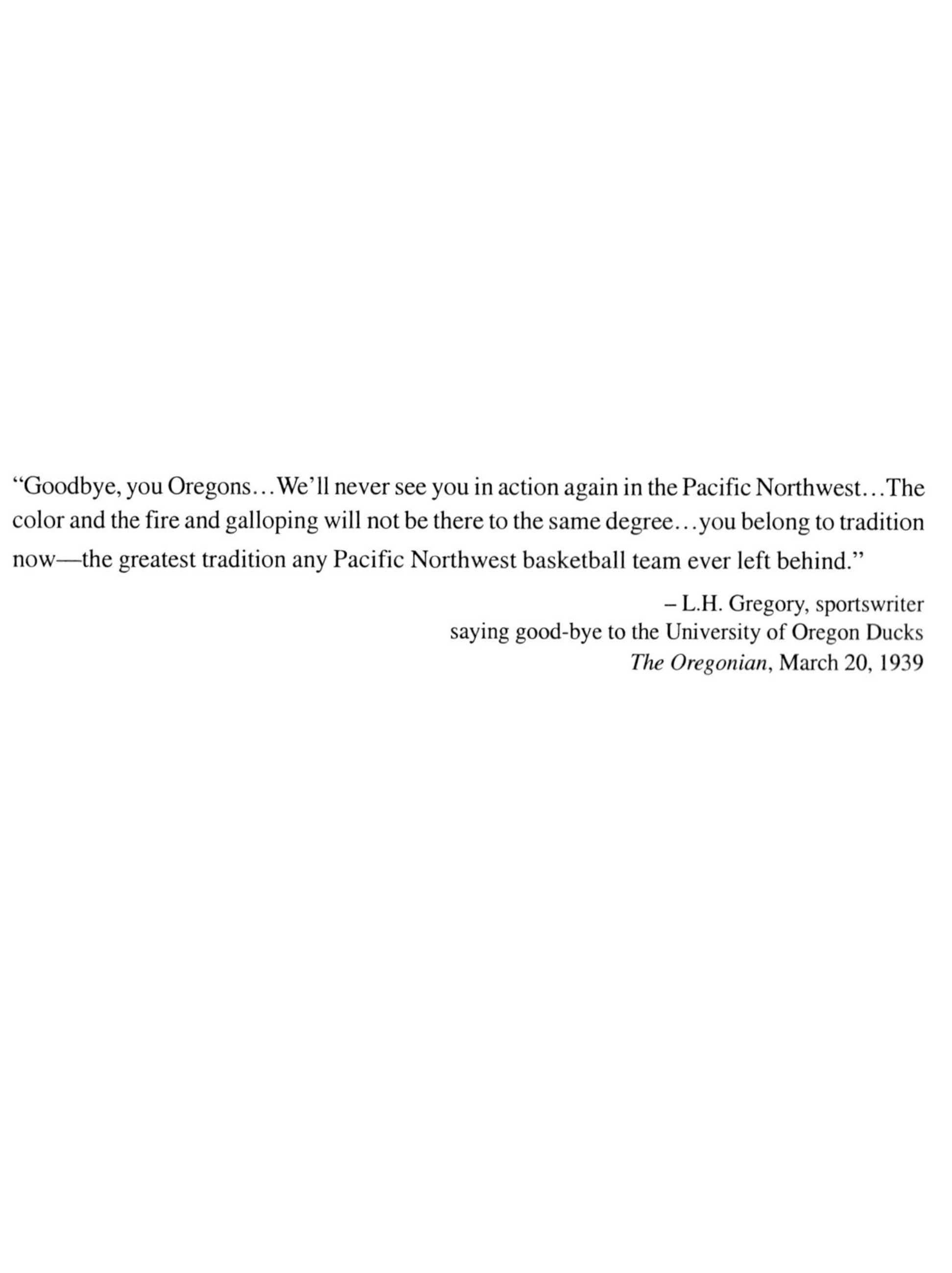

"Goodbye, you Oregons...We'll never see you in action again in the Pacific Northwest...The color and the fire and galloping will not be there to the same degree...you belong to tradition now—the greatest tradition any Pacific Northwest basketball team ever left behind."

– L.H. Gregory, sportswriter
saying good-bye to the University of Oregon Ducks
The Oregonian, March 20, 1939

Contents

Astoria
Longview
WASHINGTON
Columbia River
Portland
OREGON
Willamette River
Salem
Corvallis
Eugene
Oakridge
Washington
OREGON

A NORTHWEST TEAM

No better game was ever created for the sunshine-deprived souls of the rain-drenched Northwest than the one invented by James Naismith in 1891—basketball. Boys from northwest Oregon and southwest Washington took to the new game as ducks do to water.

In 1935 some of the basketball heroes in the region's communities began gathering on the University of Oregon campus, situated in the Willamette Valley town of Eugene, a sleepy logging and farming community located approximately sixty miles from the Pacific Ocean and about the same distance from the summit of the Cascade Range.

At this time, the University of Oregon Ducks had been coached by Bill Reinhart, who had compiled an overall record of 174–101 during twelve seasons. Yet now he was leaving for George Washington University, where he would fulfill his "long standing wish to be a head football coach." Reinhart, however, left behind the seeds of a growing basketball tradition at Oregon.

For example, when Reinhart began his career with the Ducks, Oregon played at the old Armory building; when he left, they played at McArthur Court, one the finest gyms on the West coast in the 1930s. Constructed in

Photo courtesy University of Oregon Athletic Media Services

The University of Oregon's McArthur Court

1926–27 and named for 1901 alumnus and athletic booster Clifton McArthur, the gym seated about 6,000 and was nicknamed "The Igloo" for its white concrete walls and doomed roof. Years later it would be dubbed "The Pit," though most Duck fans still know it affectionately as Mac Court.

Consequently, in the spring of 1935 Eugene had a great basketball facility surrounded by a small but growing college and a dedicated community bent on making the university's basketball teams among the finest in the nation. Luckily, two very able and successful men applied for Rinehart's job, both University of Oregon graduates.

One candidate was John Warren (class of 1928), the coach of Astoria High School, where in seven seasons his teams had won the state championship *four* times from 1930 to 1935. The other leading applicant was Howard Hobson (class of 1926), former captain of the Ducks' baseball and basketball teams during his university years, and then a successful coach at the high school level in Portland as well as at Southern Oregon Normal School in Ashland, Oregon.

With two admirable applicants to choose from, the Executive Council of the Associated Students, which was responsible for making the decision, offered the job of varsity coach to Hobson and that of freshman coach to Warren. Both were well aware of the need for recruiting and were determined to find the best talent in the Northwest.

Howard Hobson

In addition, Hobson knew that winning games required the tallest players possible, for the rules of the day favored height: limiting players to three seconds in the key, for example, and placing one offensive man under the basket during free throws. But the most significant advantage occurred during the center jump (referred to by many as the "tip off").

According to the center jump rule, after each basket a referee took the ball back to center court for a re-jump. One reason for it, wrote L.H. Gregory, sports columnist for *The Oregonian*, was that it "provided a dramatic pause after a basket."

Another reason for the rule, some argued, was that the slower tempo helped officials. "We have to keep running from one side of the court to the other," said one New York referee, "and we have a hard time getting down to the end of the court."

Still others claimed that without the center jump rule, there would be an unfair "premium on speed," and that continuous play might hurt high school players by wearing them out, even stunting their growth.

No matter the reason, one thing was certain-the rule was a major reason that scores in the early 1930s often fell below twenty points, and that the team with the taller center had the advantage when it came to controlling the ball. (Some estimated this advantage to be six to ten points per game.) It was a situation that had coaches trying to speed up the game, to increase the scoring and make it more exciting.

One popular solution was the fast break. After the center jump scramble, an intercepted pass or a rebound, players dribbled and passed as fast as possible toward their basket. Well aware of the dissatisfaction with the center jump rule, both Hobson and Warren reasoned that some day the rule would be removed, and the fast break would become the style of the future. Its only impediment then would be what some called the "dreaded stall," because once the ball crossed mid-court in the allotted ten seconds, the team in possession had no time limit on how long they could hold it before shooting.

The new Ducks' coach also needed a captain who could run the team from the floor, for the coach was restricted from communicating with the team except at halftime. Even substitutes sent into the game were not permitted to communicate with fellow players for fear they might bring in instructions from the coach.

And so with these ideas firmly in mind, Howard Hobson and John Warren began their search of Northwest high schools for basketball players.

John Warren

For the people of Astoria, Oregon—located near the confluence of the Columbia River and the Pacific Ocean, deluged with incessant rain and besieged by heavy winds—basketball was an escape from the dark months of winter. For this reason, the gymnasium on the second floor of the hilltop high school was one of the most important and most popular places in town.

Dubbed the Fighting Fishermen, Astoria achieved remarkable success on the basketball court under the guidance of John Warren, and it was here that the Ducks found two of its future players: 5-foot 8-inch senior guard Bobby Anet, an excellent passer, aggressive dribbler, and effective playmaker who helped control the tempo of the game; and 5-foot 11-inch guard Wally Johansen, an excellent ball handler and outside shooter. Together they led Astoria to the state championship in 1935, and then followed their coach to the University of Oregon.

Two future UO Ducks:
Bobby Anet (above)
Wally Johansen (below)

Perhaps the Fishermen's most formidable opponents during the 1935 season lived sixty miles to the east and across the Columbia River in the small logging town of Longview, Washington. "One of the toughest quintets those Astoria Fishermen ever played," Warren said of his teams' former rivals.

A major reason for that toughness was Longview's 6-foot 8-inch center Urgel (Slim) Wintermute, probably the tallest man in Northwest basketball, and a future dominant force for the Ducks. Even though the Portland-born Wintermute had already made a commitment to play for Slats Gil at Oregon State College, several factors persuaded him to change his mind.

One of these was the fact that Wintermute's high school coach was Scott Milligan, a former basketball star for the Ducks. Another was that he was familiar with Astorians John Warren, Bobby Anet, and Wally Johansen. In addition, even though colleges gave no scholarships in those days, Hobson was able to find jobs for Wintermute's mother as well as for Slim himself. (Slim's father had been killed in an accident.)

Meanwhile, Hobson's recruiting efforts took him on a forty-mile drive southeast of Eugene to Oakridge, a small school whose star was 6-foot 4-inch Lauren (Laddie) Gale, a first team all-state center who could shoot with either hand—hands so large he could palm the ball. Even though Gale, like Wintermute, had already been recruited by Slats Gil, some coaxing from Hobson and Gilbert Sprague—Gale's high school coach and a University of Oregon graduate—turned Gale toward Oregon. With the addition of Gale, Hobson had secured the nucleus for a basketball team that within four years would make American sports history.

Because freshmen were not permitted to play varsity basketball, the future Tall Firs went to work for John Warren on the freshman team. "All players on the frosh team," Warren warned, "would be treated equally, and those that played the best basketball would be on the team."

But to toughen Slim Wintermute and give him needed competition, Hobson had the freshman center practice with the varsity and held him out of freshman games. The coach felt it would better prepare his tallest player for his role next year as the Ducks' center. Even with Wintermute's absence, the freshman team finished its 1935-1936 season at 19–1, the best frosh record in years. (The only blemish was a 37–35 loss to Oregon State.)

The freshman sometimes performed even better than the Ducks varsity. For example, after the varsity lost 47–46 to the Riggs All-Stars, a business-sponsored team, in November, the frosh beat the same team 45–41 six weeks later. Then came a harbinger of things to come: In a January practice game, the frosh team beat the varsity.

Coach Hobson's varsity had not done so well against the Oregon State Beavers, who won three of four games against the Ducks during the 1935-36 season. And even though the Ducks finished their season with a conference record of 7-9—winding up in fourth place in the Northern Division—their overall record was 20-11, and Hobson and Warren came out of the season optimistic about the future.

During the University of Oregon's championship season, graduates of Astoria High School played key roles. Shown here with the school's 1935 state championship team—under coach John Warren, Astoria won *four* state championships between 1930 and 1935—are future Ducks Bobby Anet (front row, far left), Ted Sarpola (front, second from right) and Wally Johansen (front, far right). Their coach, John Warren (back row, far left) would go on to coach the university's freshman team and later become the Ducks' head coach. Earl Sandness, not pictured here, became the fourth Astorian to make up the Ducks' eleven-man varsity during the 1939 season.

The 1936–37 Season

As he prepared for the 1936–37 season, the soft-spoken, analytical innovator and coach "Hobby" Hobson eagerly waited for four of his players to become eligible for his varsity team: Bobby Anet, Wally Johansen, Slim Wintermute, and Laddie Gale. But to bolster his squad, he also brought in a new crop of Northwest recruits, including Evert (Red) McNeeley of Portland; Ford Mullen of Olympia, Washington; Matt Pavalunas of Raymond, Washington; Robert Hardy of Ashland, Oregon, who had transferred from Southern Oregon Normal; and Ted Sarpola and Earl Sandness of Astoria, who had both set scoring records at the state tournament and were now following their former coach, John Warren, to Eugene.

The arrival of the new season found sophomores Anet, Johansen, Wintermute, and Gale challenging the older varsity players, which consisted of seniors Ken Purdy, Bill Courtney, and captain John Lewis; and juniors Dave Silver and Ray Jewel.

The Ducks started fast, winning three straight games against business-sponsored teams before facing the UCLA Bruins of the Pacific Coast Conference, which was made up of two divisions: the Northern Division, consisting of the University of Oregon, Oregon State College, the University of Washington, Washington State College, and the University of Idaho; and the Southern Division, composed of Stanford, the University of Southern California (USC), the University of California at Los Angeles (UCLA), and the University of California. Once the two divisions had each established a winner, the two teams played for the Pacific Coast Conference championship.

At this time, a rule change affected college basketball across the nation: Incoming substitutes could now communicate with other players, which meant the coach could send in instructions. A second, experimental change would affect only the Southern Division of the Pacific Coast Conference: the elimination of the center jump rule. Consequently, Oregon's Hobson and UCLA's Caddy Works devised a scheme in which the first half of their scheduled game would be played according to the rules of the Southern Division, and the second half according to those of the Northern.

For Hobson it was probably a dream come true, since he had been advocating the fast break—and coaching his teams to run it—for many seasons. Thus when the opportunity arrived, the Ducks were ready. But so were the Bruins, who also used the fast break. In addition, Works' team boasted lanky all-star center John Ball. Yet in the first half of the game at Mac Court, the Ducks' offense exploded. Led by Slim Wintermute, who dominated the game while holding Ball to just five points, the young team gained a halftime lead of 30–17 and went on to win easily 56–30.

Following their victory, the Ducks played four games in five days—winning against Southern Oregon Normal and Chico State, but losing to Santa Clara and the University of California—before returning to Eugene, where they won two of three pre-conference games and prepared for the beginning of their conference schedule. To the amazement of many, in the first two games of that schedule the Ducks split with the Washington State Cougars, the favorites to win the division.

Laddie Gale

"Ducks break even in two games with Washington State," reported the *Oregon Daily Emerald, the university's newspaper*. "[Junior Dave Silver and Bobby Anet] lead Hobson's crew to 43–22 victory." With the win, it became evident this young Duck squad would contend for the division championship.

Using a fast break offense and a zone defense—but still forced to use the center jump—the Ducks went on to defeat Oregon State 35–34 when guard Ken Purdy hit a mid-court shot at the buzzer. Laddie Gale, however, had broken a finger in the game and would be out of action until the later part of the season.

Also hurting the team was the fact that several players were suffering from colds. Nevertheless, the Ducks hit the road for games against Washington State and Idaho, winning three of four contests. Then it was back to Eugene for a two-game home stand against the Washington Huskies. After winning the first game and losing the second, the Ducks found themselves in second place in the division, and two of its players—Slim Wintermute and Dave Silver—leading the conference's scorers.

Next up was Oregon State, and Slats Gil's "dreaded stall" offense and zone defense could not hold back the fast break and long set shots of Hobson's Ducks, who won 44–31, staying in the race for the division's top spot. Their next opponent, the Idaho Vandals, had lost all seven of their league contests, but the Ducks found them to be anything but pushovers.

"Oregon's youthful in-and-out basketeers, who are bearcats of the maple court on some occasions but plain alley cats on others," wrote *The Oregonian's* L.H. Gregory, "suffered acute spasms of alley catitis tonight, and Idaho's tail-end Vandals took the basketball game, 35–31."

The next evening was different; the Ducks returned to their "Bearcat" form and amid a combined total of forty-three personal fouls—twenty-two against Idaho, twenty-one against Oregon, and two technical fouls leveled against each team for talking back to officials—Oregon won the game 46–33, putting the Ducks back into second place.

Desperately wanting to displace the Ducks in the league standings were the Beavers of Oregon State. Near the end of February they got their chance. Playing in Corvallis, Ken Purdy again displayed great marksmanship with his long set shots, and when Wintermute fouled out, the now-healed Laddie Gale took up the slack at center. Oregon's 33–26 victory, combined with Washington's win over Washington State, put the Ducks in first place in the division title race.

Even though the next night's game found Purdy missing his long shots, the shooting, ball handling, and rebounding of sophomores Anet, Johansen, Gale, and Wintermute led the Ducks to another victory over the Beavers. It was Oregon's first four-game sweep against Oregon State since 1921.

Because Oregon and Washington both had division-leading 10–4 records, either team could win the Northern Division Championship by sweeping the two-game series. But if the teams split the series and Washington State, who was playing Oregon State at Pullman, beat the Beavers, the result would be a three-way tie for first. Hobson, however, was confident.

To see the team off to Seattle in early March, university students, townspeople, and the university band gathered at the Southern Pacific Railroad station to "entrain Coach Hobson and the team for the first Oregon championship series since 1927." And when the northbound train pulled out of the Eugene station and headed for Seattle, it left behind a cheering crowd.

When the Huskies and Ducks took the floor, Washington's 10,000-seat Pavilion was filled beyond capacity, and the two fast breaking teams collided head on. But it was a collision that saw the Huskies run over the Ducks 42–

25. Washington scored sixteen times from the field to Oregon's eight, and the Ducks' high scorers, Silver and Wintermute, put in just seven points each.

"They simply had one of those nights," L.H. Gregory wrote, "when they couldn't have hit the full moon with a five barreled shotgun."

The next night, in front of 9,000 mostly-Washington fans, the Ducks jumped out to an 8–0 lead as Wintermute repeatedly controlled the center jump against the Huskies' smaller Dick Voelker. Washington eventually pulled even with just three minutes left in the game. Then Johansen passed to Gale, who scored to put the Ducks back in front 39–37.

But with a minute left to play, Gale fouled Washington's Gannon, who made his free throw, narrowing the Ducks' lead to a point. The subsequent center jump found the Huskies controlling the ball and dribbling downcourt. The pass went to Washington's Wagner, who missed a long shot, but the Huskies took the rebound, and Egge shot. The ball took a high bounce off the rim, and Anet came up with the rebound.

Anet dribbled all over the court, between and around Washington players, until the clock wound down to fifteen seconds. Then he fired the ball to Gale, who shot. The ball wobbled around the rim and started to fall off—but then Slim Wintermute tipped it in at the buzzer, giving Oregon a 41–38 win.

The Ducks' split, along with Washington State's two wins over Oregon State, put the division race into a three-way tie, forcing a playoff involving Oregon, Washington, and Washington State, each

Slim Wintermute

with an 11–5 record. A drawing determined who played the first game in the playoff: Washington and Washington State, with the winner then playing Oregon, which had drawn a bye. So while the Cougars played the Huskies in Seattle, Oregon waited.

Because they had beaten the Cougars in three of four games that season and had the home court advantage, the Huskies were the favorites. In fact, they had lost only one home game to the Cougars in the previous seventeen years. Washington State, however, overcame the odds, the seventeen-year jinx, and a nine-point halftime deficit to walk away with a 36–33 victory. They next faced the Ducks in Pullman, with the winner going on to play Stanford for the Pacific Coast title.

It wasn't even close. Even though the Ducks trailed at the half by just a point, its defense broke down in the second half, and Wintermute was held to a total of just three points as the Cougars won 42–35. This ended the Ducks quest for a Northern Division crown. (Stanford would beat Washington State in two games, 31–28 and 41–40, winning the conference championship for the second consecutive year.)

Oregon's young team of mostly sophomores, however, had finished the season with a 20–9 record. And even though John Lewis, Ken Purdy, and Bill Courtney were ending their playing days at Oregon, Bobby Anet, Wally Johansen, Laddie Gale, Dave Silver—the only Duck named to the Northern Division All-Conference team—and Slim Wintermute were all coming back.

The 1937–38 Season

With the return of all-Northern Division forward Dave Silver, junior guards Bobby Anet (now the team captain) and Wally Johansen, forward Laddie Gale, and center Slim Wintermute, the Ducks were poised to challenge for the division title. In addition, the team had one of the strongest benches in the league with Ray Jewel, Robert Hardy, Ted Sarpola, Matt Pavalunas, John Dick, and Ford Mullen.

Also strengthening the young team at the beginning of the new season was a major change that would affect college basketball in general and the University of Oregon Ducks in particular: the complete elimination of the center jump rule. By a 60–9 vote, the National Collegiate Basketball Coaches Association had rid the game of the practice because doing so "speeded up the game, added five to six actual playing minutes, increased scoring ten percent, and reduced injuries suffered in the inevitable player jam after the Jump."

Many of the nation's coaches noted an additional change. "The game without the center jump," said Indiana University coach Everett S. Dean, "takes away some of the power of the big man."

For the University of Oregon, the repercussions were enormous. In spite of the advantage that Wintermute's height had given the Ducks the previous season, removing the center jump was like opening the floodgates to Howard Hobson's fast break style of play, and only the "dreaded stall" remained an obstacle.

To improve the speed of his players, Hobson temporarily turned the team's training over to Oregon track coach Bill Hayward, who ran the basketball players through a specially designed course of hurdles that he progressively placed closer and closer together. After his players had completed their time with Hayward, Hobson knew he had one of the fastest teams in the league.

Now able to use their speed and ball handling the entire length of the court, the young, mostly junior team plowed through their pre-season games with eleven victories, and were then ready to begin their conference schedule. With the addition of the University of Montana Grizzlies to the Northern Division, that schedule had grown from sixteen to twenty games, with each of the six teams playing every other team four times.

Photo courtesy University of Oregon Athletic Media Services

Laddie Gale

In the first of those games, back to back contests against Washington State, Anet and Johansen led the charge from the backcourt, and Laddie Gale dropped in fourteen points as the Ducks defeated the Cougars 54–33. (After the game, students attended the "Hobson Hobble," a dance dedicated to Howard Hobson.)

The next evening wasn't as easy, but Oregon prevailed again, winning by a score of 50–46. Laddie Gale's nineteen points made him high scorer, while Dave Silver contributed eleven.

But in the next game, played before a capacity crowd at Mac Court, Oregon's fast break ran into Oregon State's stall, and the Beavers put the brakes on at both ends of the court by holding the ball for as long as five minutes at a time. During one tedious stretch, a sportswriter reported, Oregon State "whipped [the ball] back and forth exactly 34 times before attempting a shot, displaying an offense so boring that it never lifted the spectators from their seats."

With Dave Silver out with chicken pox, Bob Hardy, Ted Sarpola, and John Dick rotated at one forward position. At one point, the Beavers' Kebbe slammed into Hardy, knocking Hardy to the floor and breaking his leg, an injury that put him out for most of the season. Still, the Ducks shot eighteen of twenty-one from the free throw line, and won 38–32. In addition, Gale's eleven points put him on track to break the division's scoring record, held by Oregon State's Wally Palmberg.

It was after this game that sportswriter L.H. Gregory gave the Ducks the nickname "Tall Firs," which would follow the team through the years. "The only way Oregon's tall-fir basketeers can fumble that basketball title now," Gregory wrote, "is to become falling pines at Corvallis tonight, and they're so far and away the league's best team that this just isn't a reasonable thought." Yet Gregory's prophesy missed the mark.

Oregon's second game against the Beavers, played in Corvallis, was a repeat of the first, with the Beavers' slow pace and tight defense choking the Ducks' fast break, and this time the Beavers won 36–32.

Putting the loss behind them, the Ducks returned home and resumed their winning ways, defeating Montana twice, 69–43 and 54–42, with Johansen, Anet, and Gale each scoring in double figures.

From here the Ducks hit the road for a five-day, four-game schedule against Washington and Montana. During their 1,600-mile trip, Oregon broke even, splitting against both schools. In spite of the break-even record, Hobson was pleased with his team's performance. "They kept driving and they didn't let a defeat get them to downhearted," he said.

"They kept coming back harder than ever in the second game of both series to win." In addition, Hobson called the play of juniors Anet, Johansen, Gale, and Wintermute "outstanding."

It was this kind of performance that put the Ducks at the top of the division standings—but then they ran full-tilt into a six game series to be played over nine days in February. They began at home by defeating Washington 59–43 and 56–53, then traveled to Idaho for two games.

The strategy of Idaho coach Forrest Twogood was simple: hold on to the ball as long as possible. The stall worked. Idaho controlled the ball for two-thirds of the game, and Oregon couldn't get its fast break going as the Ducks lost 33–28.

In the second game, Laddie Gale needed just six points to break the division's season scoring record, but the Vandals double-teamed him, guarding him so closely it made it difficult for him to score—but easier for others. Instead of shooting, Gale passed to Wintermute, whose size overpowered the Vandals. The half ended with the Ducks leading 22–14, but halftime found Wintermute crippled with stomach cramps and unable to play.

Without Wintermute's dominance beneath the basket, Idaho regained control, but as soon as the Vandals tied the score at 23, Wintermute emerged from the locker room and re-entered the game. The lead went back and forth until Idaho led 32–30 with fifty second left to play. Then Gale was fouled. His two successful free throws not only tied the game, but also gave him the division's scoring record.

But then with one second left on the clock, Gale fouled Idaho's Willis Bowman, who made his free throw to give the Vandals a 33–32 win. With Oregon's loss, Washington State took over at the top of the standings, and the Ducks dropped into a tie for second with Idaho. It was obvious that the division was probably as competitive as it had ever been.

“We have Oregon with its fast break, hard running style,” Vandal coach Forrest Twogood said in analyzing the division. “Washington with fast running and fast passing; Washington State and its close checking, fast passing and constant shooting; Oregon State with its tight zone defense and checking, along with a slow breaking style that’s just the reverse of Oregon’s, and then our own club with its emphasis on defensive checking and offensive ball handling.”

On Valentine’s Day 1938, two days after their loss to Idaho, the Ducks were in Pullman to take on the “close checking” Washington State Cougars. Oregon split the two-game series, as they did the six games of the road trip, and the losses dropped them to third place with four games left in the season.

In Eugene they beat Idaho twice and Oregon State once, then traveled to Corvallis for the last conference game of the year—and they had to beat the Beavers to have a chance of winning the Northern Division title. (Washington also had to beat Washington State at least once in Seattle.) Once again, it came down to the Ducks’ fast break against the Beavers’ stall.

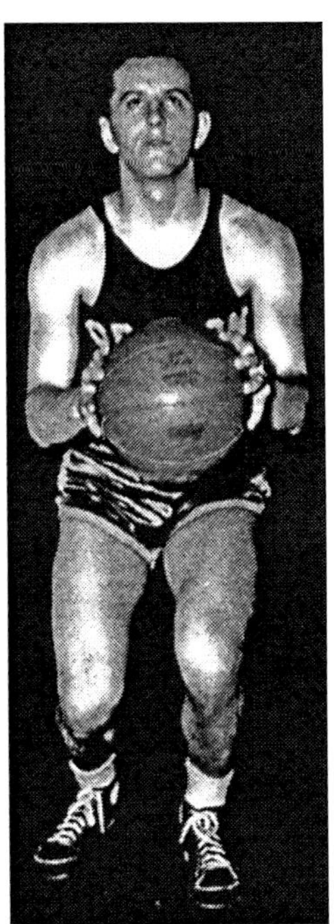

Bobby Anet

After swapping leads throughout the first half, the Beavers went into the locker room at halftime leading 15–13. The lead continued to see-saw through the second half until, with less than eight minutes left in the game and the Ducks trailing 27–26, Wintermute fouled out. But instead of folding, the Ducks got tougher.

The turning point seemed to come when Anet made two free throws to put Oregon in the lead by a point. Then Dave Silver connected on two consecutive baskets, making the score 32–27. Finally, Anet scored on a rebound shot to increase the lead to seven points.

Wally Johansen

Oregon State made a run in the last few minutes, closing the gap to just one point. But the Ducks stalled and the Beavers fouled, and first John Dick and then Laddie Gale scored free throws to put the game out of reach. In this last conference game, Anet and Johansen were the high scorers with ten points each.

"The tall boys have their 'on' nights when they roll up huge scoring totals and are unbeatable," L.H. Gregory wrote, "and also their 'off' ones, when they can't seem to hit a lick, as in the final Corvallis game. But Anet and Johansen are the same last night, tonight, and tomorrow night."

Meanwhile, in Seattle, Washington twice defeated Washington State, so the Ducks victory over the Beavers gave Oregon—now 14–6 in conference play—the division championship, their first in eleven years. They would now play 10–2 Stanford for the Pacific Coast Conference championship.

A major reason for the Stanford Indian's success was Hank Luisetti, considered by most sports writers of the day to be the best basketball player ever to don a uniform. Using his revolutionary one-handed set shot—in an age dominated by the two-handed set shot and the two-handed, between-the-knees free throw—Luisetti had set an all time collegiate scoring record of 1,550 points. So complete was Luisetti's dominance of the game that some believed that he made Stanford unbeatable—but Howard Hobson thought otherwise.

Apparently, so did the huge crowd of supporters that gave the Ducks a rip-roaring send off as the team left Eugene on the Southern Pacific, traveling south to California for their meeting with one of the finest teams—and perhaps the best player—in the nation. The eleven Oregon players on board were Bobby Anet, Wally Johansen, Slim Wintermute, Laddie Gale (recovering from a back injury he had sustained in the last game with Oregon State), Dave Silver, Ray Jewel, Ford Mullen, John Dick, Matt Pavalunas, Ted Sarpola, and Robert Hardy, wrapped with "a pound of tape on his injured leg."

Of these, Gale, Wintermute, and Johansen had all been chosen for the All-Northern Division team—as voted by ten varsity players from each team and six coaches from the division—and Laddie Gale, who had scored more than four hundred points during the season, was voted the division's most valuable player.

On arriving in San Francisco, the Ducks found that one of the championship's main attractions was the match-up between Hank Luisetti and their own Laddie Gale. Yet Hobson knew his team was better than any single player.

"Hobby Hobson grins as he recalls the effectiveness of his other boys," wrote Vincent Gates of Eugene's *Register-Guard*, "Wintermute, Silver, Sarpola, Anet, Johansen, Dick and Pavalunas. Stanford, he muses, has Luisetti, I have five of them. The meaning is clear. If Gale is pinned down and watched like a hawk...the rest of the Ducks are quite capable of scoring."

But it was still difficult to overcome Luisetti, who lived up to his reputation by scoring twenty points in the first game and twenty-six in the second, leading Stanford to two wins by scores of 52–39 and 59–51. (Gale scored twelve points in the first game and eighteen in the second.)

It was Luisetti's last college game, which meant the Ducks—with four of their starters returning, losing only All-Coast forward Dave Silver from the ten-man rotation—had an even better shot at next season's title. After all, as Idaho coach Forrest Twogood pointed out, "Stanford won't always have a Hank Luisetti."

Besides Luisetti, Stanford was also losing three other starters as well as coach John Bunn, who had led the Indians for thirty-eight seasons. (He was also the man who said, "Tall guys are not good basketball players.")

In addition, the young Oregon team came away from their defeat with a new sense of fight. "After the Ducks lost the PCC title series to Stanford in 1938," team member John Dick said forty years later, "we gathered in a huddle and vowed that we'd win this thing the following year and if there was a national championship, we'd win that, too."

And the following year, there *would* be a national championship, the first ever for collegiate basketball.

The 1938–39 Season

The beginning of the new basketball season brought with it a revolutionary idea in collegiate sports: a national basketball championship sponsored by the National College Athletic Association (NCAA), with the winner determined by a series of playoff tournaments held across the country.

Prior to this, the highest honor for any college basketball team was an invitation to the National Invitation Tournament held in March at New York's Madison Square Garden, where some of the finest teams in the land played in front of crowds numbering as many as 18,000. Ned Irish, a former New York sportswriter, organized this tournament, as well as a winter tournament he called "Double Headers" because of its schedule of back-to-back games.

Seeing the huge profit made from these privately-promoted tournaments, Harold G. Olsen, coach at Ohio State University, submitted to the National Association of Basketball Coaches (NABC) a plan that had the NCAA sponsoring a national tournament. At first the idea didn't receive much support, but Olsen persisted. Finally, in October of 1938, the NCAA endorsed the idea with the condition that the NABC handle the tournament. As a result, the coaching organization began laying plans for the first NCAA basketball championship.

First the coaches divided the United States into eight geographical districts, with each district represented by the region's conference winners. For the four districts located east of the Mississippi River, the playoffs would be held in Philadelphia; for the four districts west of the Mississippi, in San Francisco. The two regional winners would then meet in the championship game, the first of which would be held on March 27, 1939, at Evanston, Illinois.

In the meantime, the winter tournament in New York went on as usual, and this year the University of Oregon had been invited after impressing promoter Ned Irish with its Northern Division championship last year and its 4–0 start this season. Responsible for that winning streak was the Ducks' core of formidable seniors: the scoring of forward Laddie Gale, the division's all time leading scorer and a unanimous choice on last year's conference all star team; the inside dominance of center Slim Wintermute, last season named as an all star to the division's first team and the conference's second team; and, of course, the ball handling and outside shooting of guards Bobby Anet and Wally Johansen.

"They drive ceaselessly and mercilessly, no matter what the situation," L.H. Gregory wrote of the Duck guards, "and they never seem to slow up. They're the spark for the big boys. So far as I can see, they're always good."

Because Dave Silver was the only starter the team had lost to graduation, three players were competing for his forward position: 6-foot 2-inch junior Ted Sarpola, a former three-time all-state player from Astoria High School who had set several state tournament scoring records; 6-foot 4 inch sophomore Earl Sandness, another all-state, high-scoring Astorian; and 6-foot 3-inch senior Robert (Ollie) Hardy, a transfer from Southern Oregon College who had been a scoring threat for his former school.

The balance of the team consisted of 6-foot 4-inch junior center John Dick, an excellent defensive player from The Dalles who had a whirling pivot shot that was just about unstoppable; 6-foot 2-inch sophomore Evert

McNeeley; 6-foot junior Matt Pavalunas; 5-foot 8-inch junior Ford Mullen, and Donald Mabee.

And so on a December evening in 1938, Coach Hobby Hobson and his twelve-man team embarked on a three week, nine game barnstorming tour to the east coast. Their first stop was Madison Square Garden in New York City.

Bobby Anet on program

From the beginning, the Ducks faced long odds in their first game against the City College of New York (CCNY) Beavers. After a cross-country trip of 3,000 miles, they were playing in an unfamiliar gym against a bigger school, one with a student population of more than ten times that of the Oregon's approximately 3,000. In addition, they were playing a team that used a different style of play. According to the *Register Guard's* Dick Strite, this involved some rough play.

"Little things that are used to break thc stride of hard charging forwards," Strite wrote, "a little side-swipe here and there to make a shot go just a bit out of line—not personal fouls that are noticeable to most officials...but still deliberate fouls...boys on the [Pacific] coast aren't taught that kind of basketball."

To make matters worse, Wintermute and Gale were fighting colds. Even so, Oregon's height advantage and its unblemished record prompted the *New York Times* to make the Ducks the favorite. But at the beginning of the game at Madison Square Garden, played in front of a sold-out crowd of more than 16,000, the Ducks received a warning about the kind of night they were in for.

"Now we aren't going to call every little brush a foul," official Pat Kenedy said to Hobson before the game. "That's okay with you, isn't it?"

Although he agreed, Hobson got more than he bargained for. The Beavers of CCNY, he said later, "stepped on your feet, grabbed your pants, and the officials allowed more contact on the screens."

Hampered by the lenient officiating as well as the rough play of its smaller opponents, the fast breaking Ducks went scoreless in the first fifteen minutes, though they eventually closed the gap to trail at the half 19–14.

After regaining their composure, the Ducks came out in the second half and made a game of it. Bobby Anet's free throw and Wally Johansen's two-pointer tied the score at 30. But with eight minutes left in the game, CCNY scored five straight points before Oregon narrowed the score to 37–36. Anet missed a free throw that would have tied the score, but CCNY made a free throw and then finished out the game with a mid-court stall to win 38–36.

Over the next twelve days, the Ducks traveled almost 2,000 miles across the East and Midwest to play some of the region's best teams in another segment of an overall journey described by forward John Dick as "Shake, rattle and roll."

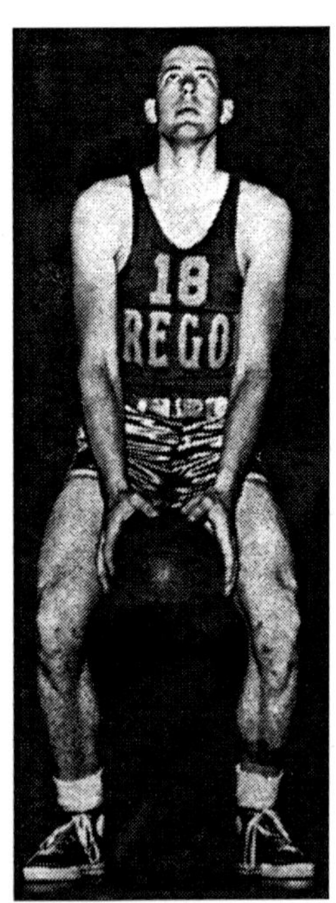

John Dick

In Philadelphia they defeated St. Joseph 54–44; in Cleveland, Miami of Ohio, 74–38, a game in which Wintermute suffered a sprained ankle, putting backup center John Dick into the lineup; in Buffalo, Canisius College, 53–41; and in Detroit, Wayne University, 52–41, with Wally Johansen scoring fourteen points and John Dick nine.

Then it was on to Peoria, Illinois, where the Ducks' winning streak was broken. Even though Laddie Gale led all scorers with fourteen points, Bradley Tech took a 52–39 victory. The next night, however, Oregon got back on track in Chicago, where forward Ted Sarpola scored eighteen points to lead the Ducks to a 60–45 win over Macomb.

It was this kind of individual performance that prompted noted radio sports announcer Bill Stern to give Sarpola an unusual nickname. "He called me the 'whirling dervish,'" Sarpola said, "because I could change hands while in the act of shooting."

The Ducks continued their winning ways in Des Moines, Iowa, defeating Drake University 42–31 behind the combined twenty-two points of John Dick and Laddie Gale.

On the last day of December, two days after defeating Drake, the team headed west, traveling 1,700 railroad miles to San Francisco and their game against Stanford University, whom the Ducks had lost to in last year's Pacific Coast Conference title game. In spite of a nineteen-point performance by Gale, Stanford downed the train-weary Ducks 50–46.

Now even more weary because of their loss to Stanford, Oregon rode a Southern Pacific train six hundred miles back to Eugene, ending their barnstorming tour the day after New Year's, 1939. It had been a trip with some unexpected benefits.

"We learned to travel and change living accommodations daily and to travel up to ninety-six consecutive hours by train with no opportunity to practice or even get any meaningful exercise," said John Dick. "Perhaps most importantly, we learned to adapt quickly to officiating differences and differences in rule interpretations that varied widely from one area to another."

After 18 days, 7,000 miles, and 10 games—of which they had won 7—the Ducks had just enough time to prepare for their division opener at home against Washington State. (Montana had dropped from the division, again leaving four teams to play sixteen games each.)

Oregon took the first game 46–35, with Wintermute leading all scorers with eighteen points. The next night, however, the Cougars held Gale to a single basket and the Ducks to less than twenty percent shooting from the field to pull out a stunning 39–34 victory. It was Oregon's first loss at home in two years.

Laddie Gale

The Ducks' schedule then took them on the road, where they played five games over a span of nine days (four of those games came in only five days). The first contest was played in Corvallis, where the Ducks, in spite of the Beavers' stalling, prevailed 31–26. It was a game in which two significant developments unfolded for Oregon: Laddie Gale once again began scoring in double figures, and John Dick was winning the battle for the forward position.

In the next two games, Gale scored thirty-four points and Dick totaled twenty-two to lead the Ducks past Washington State 57–49 and 58–42, putting Oregon's division record at 4–1.

In the following series against Idaho, the Vandals tried to slow the pace of the games to neutralize the Ducks' fast break. In the first game, the lead switched hands numerous times, but the ball stealing of Anet and Johansen made the difference, and the Ducks pulled out 38–30 win. In the second game, however, it was the strength of Oregon's bench that made the difference.

With less then five minutes left in that game and Idaho leading 31–26, Oregon's Dick, Johansen, and Anet all fouled out. Off the bench came Ford Mullen and Matt Pavalunas. Idaho's Steve Belko fouled Mullen, who dropped in the free throw. Soon after, Mullen scored from the field, bringing the Ducks to within two. Idaho tried to stall but lost the ball to Oregon. Then Idaho's guard, Hopkins, fouled Laddie Gale. Soon after Gale sank the free throw, he tipped in a shot that gave the Ducks a 32–31 lead. In the last thirty seconds, Pavalunas "bagged a short one," Mullen made a free throw, and Oregon won the hard-fought contest 35–31. It was an important turning point of the season, for the bench had taken on a new and important role.

Then came Oregon State at Corvallis, a contest of poor shooting in which the Beavers connected on just fifteen of fifty-one shots (twenty-nine percent), and Oregon made only thirteen of seventy (eighteen percent). The Ducks, however made twenty of twenty-eight free throws, the difference in their 46–39 win.

With their division record at 7–1, the Ducks stood second in the standings behind Washington, whom they would face in a two-game series to be played at Mac Court. In his sixteen years as Washington's coach, Hec Edmundson had taken his Huskies to eight division and two conference titles, but he felt this year's team was his best.

Like Oregon, Washington had built its offense around the fast break, and after playing one full season without the center jump, both teams were maturing in the mastery of this new style of play that in the first game kept spectators on the edge of their seats, hardly giving them enough time to eat their popcorn, as they watched the two teams sprint from one end of the court to the other.

At halftime the Huskies led 27–24, but the Ducks returned to the court for the second half completely charged. The playing during the next four minutes and ten seconds was spectacular:

15 seconds—Wintermute scores a free throw.
45 seconds—Gale shoots one in from side court to tie the score at 27.
50 seconds—Washington's Dorsey pots one from the keyhole.
60 seconds—Bobby Anet slips under the basket and scores to tie the score at 29.
1:30—Washington's Zieganfuss hits a long set shot from side court.
1:50—Johansen hits from thirty feet out to tie the score at 31.
2:10—Washington's Mark Dorsey drops in a long shot.
2:20—John Dick rebounds and scores to tie the score at 33.
2:30—Washington drives downcourt, and Zieganfuss scores on a close-in shot.

3:30—Wintermute recovers his own missed free throw and scores from field to tie the score at 35.

4:10—John Dick drops in another basket to give Oregon the lead 37–35.

At this point, Washington called a time-out. "Edmundson had to call time-out," Hobson said, "a sign to his team that he had to concede a point of pride: It broke the Huskies spirit."

Meanwhile, the capacity crowd was emotionally drained from the intensity of the contest. "There never was such a galloping exhibition as two racing teams put on in this historic 250 seconds," L.H. Gregory wrote. "The crowd needed time out more than the players."

After the time-out, the Ducks pulled the game out of the Huskies' reach, winning 57–49.

During their next three games, the Ducks kept their momentum, beating Washington 58–42 and then Idaho 45–28 and 53–36.

With four games left to play—two each with Oregon State and Washington—the Ducks stood at the top of the Northern Division with a record of 11–1, including ten straight wins. (After losing once to Washington State, Washington was second at 8–3.)

The rivalry between Oregon and Oregon State was legendary, and their basketball games often more closely resembled football in their roughness. In every meeting between the two, injuries occurred frequently and brawls occasionally. This time was no exception. In the first meeting of the two-game series, one such fight erupted in which both Laddie Gale and Wally Johansen suffered injuries.

With two starters out, the Ducks found itself struggling to defend against the Beavers' Elmer Kolberg, a football player turned basketball guard. On this night, he couldn't seem to miss the basket. Having switched from a team that relied on the stall to one that ran the fast break, Oregon State continually passed the ball downcourt to Kolberg, who would shoot short or long, guarded or unguarded, and the ball seemed always to find the hoop.

Much to the delight of Corvallis fans, Kolberg's seventeen points led the Beavers to a 50–31 victory. "Even the best," George Pasero wrote in the *Emerald*, "must lose once in a while."

For Hobson, the loss was a simple matter. The Ducks, he said, had been "out-played and soundly beaten…but not outrun."

Bob Hardy

During the next week of practice, Hobson declared that every position on the team was up for grabs. According to both Ford Mullen and Robert Hardy, it was these practices that made the Oregon team great, with the second string players trying so hard to win a starting position that it was not uncommon by the end of a scrimmage to see blood. These scrimmages, Hardy said, were just as rough as playing Oregon State. But it was also common knowledge that Oregon's second string consisted of players good enough to start for numerous other schools around the country.

The next game against Oregon State shifted to Mac Court. For five players—Wally Johansen, Bobby Anet, Laddie Gale, Slim Wintermute, and Robert Hardy—it was not only their last home game in the Northern Division race, but also their last game against the Beavers. They made it count.

Even though Johansen played only a few minutes—he was still recovering from injuries suffered in the last game—Wintermute and Gale combined for twenty two points while Oregon State's Kolberg was held to five, and the Ducks sailed to a 48–37 win.

The division title now rested in the outcome of match up remaining in Seattle between the 12–2 Ducks and the 11–3 Huskies. One win would give the Ducks the championship, though getting that victory would require a fierce effort.

"Washington's Huskies play the hardest driving type of basketball in the league," wrote George Varnell of the *Seattle Daily Times*, "the racehorse variety featured by speed and continual driving from whistle to whistle."

Still, Hobson was confident. "I think [the Ducks] are nearer their peak now," he said, "than at any other time this season."

On a morning in early March of 1939 at Eugene's depot, a loyal gathering of Oregon fans gave the Ducks a rousing send off. Some drove to Seattle to watch the game but arrived to find the Pavilion already filled to capacity. Hundreds of people were locked out of the arena, and some tried to break in through the windows and doors. Only with the arrival of the police did the rioters quiet down. "Holders of season tickets," reported one newspaper, "were taken in through the crowd under police protection."

Even the players didn't escape the rush of the crowd. "As we neared the Pavilion about an hour before tip-off of the first game in Seattle," said forward John Dick, the only junior on Oregon's starting five, "our cabs were stopped a block or so short of the entrance by a large crowd that covered the approaches to the entry doors and spilled onto the street, blocking the flow of traffic. Security personnel were sent to escort us through the crowd into the Pavilion."

Once inside, Oregon faced an opponent with a simple, straightforward game plan. "We'll shoot the works in the first game," Hec Edmundson said. "If we can take that one, the pressure will be even up on Saturday night."

The referee threw the ball for the jump, and the game began. Both teams raced up and down the court at a frenetic pace. At the five-minute mark Washington led 5–1. Oregon began to draw closer as Gale sank a free throw and John Dick scored a two pointer from the keyhole.

At seven minutes, Johansen scored on a long shot to give Oregon a 6–5 lead. Thirty seconds later the Huskies regained the lead. For two minutes both teams engaged in their fast breaking styles with neither team scoring until Wintermute tipped in a rebound to put Oregon ahead 8–7. Then each team found its range from the field, and the half ended with Oregon ahead 19–16.

The beginning of the second half saw Washington come within a point of the Ducks, 23–22, but then Oregon went on a scoring spree, scoring eleven points to stretch their lead to 34–23.

The Huskies became desperate and lost their composure, and the Ducks walked away with a 39–26 win as well as the Northern Division title. Even though Gale (eleven points) and Wintermute (thirty-one rebounds) were the team's statistical leaders, the win was, as always, a team victory.

"I've always felt that our team's greatest strength was our closeness on and off the court," Dick said, "and our willingness to place team goals above individual ones."

The following night, in the last game of the division's regular schedule, Oregon triumphed again, this time 54–52.

What lay ahead for the Ducks was the series against the winner of the Southern Division for the conference title, an honor Oregon hadn't won since 1919. The Southern Division, however, had yet to determine its champion. The USC and the University of California had tied for their division's lead, a problem that required a three-game series between the two schools to solve. The winner would then play Oregon at Mac Court for the right to advance to the regional tournament of the first-ever NCAA championship.

Oregon's Tall Firs (from left): Bobby Anet, Laddie Gale, Slim Wintermute, John Dick, Wally Johansen

The Title Run

And so in the spring of 1939, the University of Oregon Ducks began their run for the national title.

The Conference Title

After California defeated USC 42–36 in the playoff game for the Southern Division championship, the Bears traveled to Eugene to face the Ducks in front of more than 6,000 fans at Mac Court. In the reserved section, not far from the press table, sat members of Oregon's 1919 basketball team, the only Duck team so far to win the Pacific Coast Conference title. (Coincidentally, they beat California for the crown.) Adding to the emotional setting, five seniors were set to play their last home series for the Ducks—Bobby Anet, Wally Johansen, Slim Wintermute, Laddie Gale, and Bob Hardy.

With Bobby Anet leading the fast break, Gale scored eighteen points, Wintermute eleven, and Johansen nine as Oregon won the first game of the three-game series, 54–49.

"Listen," California coach Nibs Price told Hobson at a post-game party, "we'll stop those big horses of yours tomorrow night—wait and see."

Photo courtesy University of Oregon Athletic Media Services

Inside Mac Court in the 1930s

Price wasn't kidding. The next game saw the Bears hold Gale to six free throws, though his teammates took up the slack. When John Dick's basket with eleven minutes left put Oregon ahead by one, it was a lead that the Ducks would build on, finally winning 53–47 for a two-game sweep. Even though the combined thirty-two points and thirty-one rebounds of Dick and Wintermute paced the Ducks on this night, it was Oregon's guards that made the difference.

"What really beat us was those little fellows, Anet and Johansen," said California's Price. "They were just too fast. That driving—whew! They kept mussing up our plays so that we never had a chance to set. That's what really ruined us."

As the crowd in Mac Court roared its approval, many were also saddened that this special team had just played its last home game. It was time, L.H. Gregory wrote in *The Oregonian*, to say goodbye to the "one-time alley cats of those in and out but always picturesque sophomore days of three seasons ago, but now stepping out of the Pacific Northwest basketball picture with two Northern Division titles and the championship of the Pacific Coast Conference!"

The Regional Tournament

When the Ducks left Eugene and headed toward San Francisco for the NCAA Western Regional Tournament, Bobby Anet was so sure of winning that he carried in his suitcase enough clothes for the train trip from San Francisco to Evanston, Illinois, the site of the first NCAA championship game. But before that happened, the Ducks had to win at San Francisco, where they almost immediately encountered their first obstacle—they couldn't get into the gym.

"A special bus was scheduled to pick up the Oregon team Monday night," reported a local paper. "After waiting an hour, the boys got tired and at 8:15 took taxis...At the gate, guards wouldn't allow entrance...at the Coliseum, the doorman thought it was a good gag, but strictly phony...after 20 more minutes they were convinced...and that's how Oregon played in the NCAA championships."

Once inside the gym, the Ducks made up for lost time. After appearing sluggish through much of the first half of their game with Texas, Oregon finally caught fire behind the scoring of Wintermute and Dick to take a 19–16 halftime lead and a 56–41 victory. The win set up the regional championship game against Oklahoma, which had defeated Utah State 50–39.

In that game, Oregon had an advantage in height and speed—and defense, thanks to some innovative coaching that put a wrinkle into the fact that teams at the time played either a man-to-man or a zone defense according to some preconceived expectations.

"When teams played zone," Hobson said, "they played with their hands in the air. When they played man-to-man, their arms where at their sides." Hobson's idea, however, was to play a man-to-man with hands up. "The Oklahoma players," he said, "never caught on." The result was a 55–37 Oregon victory.

Howard Hobson

"The deciding factor," reported the *Register Guard*, "seemed to be Oregon's remarkable defense. With three Oregon giants presenting a formidable wall, the Oklahoman's were forced to make most of their field tries from long range."

Those three "giants"—Wintermute, Gale, and Dick—were chosen to the tournament's all star team. And now with the Western Regional trophy in hand, the Ducks would face the eastern champions, Ohio State, in Evanston, Illinois.

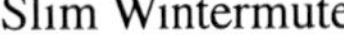

Slim Wintermute

Laddie Gale

John Dick

The National Championship

Bobby Anet's optimism in packing extra clothes paid off. On Wednesday, March 22, the Ducks left San Francisco on the Southern Pacific, and three days later they arrived in Chicago, two days before the championship game. From here they moved on to Evanston and Northwestern University, whose small, rickety gym with its raised floor would be the site of the first NCAA championship game the following Monday night.

The Ducks' opponent, the Ohio State Buckeyes, was coming into the game with a 16–6 Big Ten Conference record, and victories over Wake Forest (64–52) and Villanova (53–36) that had given them the eastern crown. Several factors seemed to make the Buckeyes favorites: They had arrived in Evanston a week prior to the game, giving them time to practice while the Ducks had been riding the train; the officials were from the Big Ten, whose rules were familiar to the Buckeyes; and the Midwestern crowd undoubtedly favored the Ohio State team.

Meanwhile, the Ducks could count Ivie Wintermute, Slim's mother, among the Oregon fans rooting for them from the stands. Mrs. Wintermute had wanted desperately to see the game, her son's last, but with the country still in the grips of the Great Depression, she didn't make enough money working at Washburne's Department Store to pay for the trip. Then the store's owners, Mr. And Mrs. Carl G. Washburne, decided to send her to the game. Before her train departed, her co-workers from Washburne's as well as members of her son's fraternity, Phi Delta Theta, gave her a surprise going away. With her friends showering her with flowers and gifts, and with her son's fraternity brothers serenading her, Mrs. Wintermute began her long journey east.

Washburne's department store was also one of the sponsors for the local broadcast of the game over Eugene's KORE radio station. According to the *Register Guard*, it was the "longest hookup (2,294 miles) for a sports event in Oregon radio history."

Among the 5,000 spectators packed into the Northwestern gym for the game were as many as 400 of the nation's college coaches who had come to see the tournament they had created; Dr. James Naismith, who had invented the game of basketball; a group of Oregon alumni from Chicago who had brought with them a small band to play the "Mighty Oregon" fight song; Oregonian Paul Jackson, who had hitchhiked from Eugene, spending six days on the road and arriving the day before the game; and, of course, Mrs. Ivie Wintermute. Otherwise, as the two teams walked to mid-court for the center jump, it was obvious that most of the crowd consisted of Ohio State fans.

Slim Wintermute faced off against 6-foot 4-inch John Schick. Referee John Getchell threw up the ball. Wintermute leaped, tapped it to an Oregon player, and the Ducks immediately took a long shot. Bobby Anet, the smallest man on the court, sprinted to the backboard, grabbed the rebound, and made the basket. (It was common to see Anet fighting for rebounds against players who dwarfed him.)

Taking possession, Ohio State began working toward its basket, but then Anet intercepted a pass and was immediately fouled. At the one minute mark, Anet sunk the free throw to make the score 3–0.

Starters in the 1939 NCAA championship game for the Ohio State Buckeyes (from left): Jim Hull, Dick Baker, John Schick, Bob Lynch, Dick Boughner

Again the Buckeyes worked toward their end of the court, trying to move against an Oregon man-to-man defense with the arms-up appearance of a zone. When the Buckeyes' long shot missed, Wintermute grabbed the rebound and passed to Anet as forwards Gale and Dick raced down the sidelines in a fast break. Anet fired a pass to John Dick, who was fouled. His free throw gave the Ducks a 4–0 lead.

University of Oregon Athletic Media Services

John Dick

Ohio State passed the ball in to captain Jim Hull, who took three short shots in a row, only to end up in a held ball with John Dick. Ohio State took possession after the jump, and the ball was passed to center John Schick, who was fouled by Wintermute. At that point, 6-foot 6-inch William Sattler, normally a center, replaced Dick Baker at forward to give the Buckeyes more height beneath the basket.

After the substitution, Schick missed his free throw, Oregon grabbed the rebound, and Johansen took the pass. He dribbled downcourt and shot from the key, his basket boosting Oregon's lead to 6–0.

With Ohio State back on offense, Hull was fouled while shooting. His first free throw missed but the second didn't—the Buckeyes' first point after almost four minutes of play. Ohio State took the rebound, and Hull's shot from the side was good.

Ohio State regained possession, and even though Hull's short shot bounced off the rim, teammate Bill Sattler's tip-in brought the Buckeyes within a point, 6-5.

Then it was Oregon's turn. Bobby Anet dribbled to mid-court, where his pass sailed into the big hands of Laddie Gale, who was fouled while shooting. His two free throws stretched the Ducks' lead to 8-5.

At their end of the court, Ohio State lost the battle for the rebound, and after Johansen brought the ball back for Oregon, he passed to Wintermute,

Wally Johansen

who was fouled. When Wintermute missed his free throw, Ohio State grabbed the rebound and passed the ball to Hull, who sunk the basket and cut Oregon's lead to 8-7.

Wally Johansen returned with the ball to his offensive zone. A threat from practically anywhere on the court, he drove from one side of the court to the other, challenging every defensive player, then quickly passed the ball into Gale, whose hook shot put the Ducks ahead 10-7 with five minutes gone in the game. Ohio State called a time out. (And the small but enthusiastic band of Oregon alumni played "Mighty Oregon.")

When play resumed, Oregon regained possession with a defensive rebound and then sped back to its end of the court. Anet faked to drive one way, then hurled the ball to John Dick, who was fouled by Hull. Dick's free throw made the score 11-7. But then Bob Lynch's long shot brought the Buckeyes back to within two.

Almost before the ball was taken out of bounds, Oregon's offense was in position beneath its basket. Anet took the pass from Johansen, dribbled past the center line, faked one way and then passed another to Gale, who was fouled by Sattler. Gale's free throw made the score 12-9, but then the Buckeyes' Lynch scored to whittle the Ducks' lead to 12–11 with ten minutes gone in the game.

Then it was Johansen and Anet for the Ducks, each scoring twice to push the lead to 18–11; then Hull scored from the field for the Buckeyes; Dick from the free throw line and then from the field for the Ducks; Hull, again from the field; and Mickelson from the free throw line for the Buckeyes' to end the half with the Ducks leading 21–16.

"As the teams went down to the dressing rooms," Hobson later recalled, "Ohio State captain Jimmy Hull said loudly, 'We'll run them into the ground in the second half,' to which Wally Johansen replied, 'I wish they'd run a little so we could work up a sweat…they play so slow that they're almost permanent fixtures of the court.'"

Meanwhile, the Ducks' size and speed were impressing those seeing it for the first time. "Oregon was surprisingly fast for such a big team," said a United Press correspondent. "The Buckeyes expected to rush the [Oregon] zone defense before it could get set and found that by the time [Ohio State] reached offensive territory, the zone already had formed. They could do nothing with it and banked mostly on long shots." (Even the sports writers didn't realize that Hobson's defense was not a zone.)

At the jump to begin the second half, Wintermute tapped the ball to Anet, and Oregon went on offense. An outside shot missed, Ohio State rebounded, and Hull made a quick basket to bring the Buckeyes to within three, 21–18.

Anet took the inbounds pass, dribbled downcourt, and chucked the ball to Gale, who missed the short shot. Again Ohio State came up with the rebound, and again it was Hull who scored. Less than a minute into the half, the Ducks' lead had slipped to 21–20.

After taking the inbounds pass, Anet raced past mid-court and drove for the basket, drawing Ohio State defenders away from Wintermute and leaving the center open for a second. And in that second, Anet's pass found the big center, who scored.

Bobby Anet

Oregon's 23–20 lead remained for several minutes while the ball changed hands several times with neither team able to score. Finally, at the defensive end of the court, Wintermute took a rebound, passed it to Anet, and the Ducks' fast break erupted. Anet found Gale, whose basket widened the lead to 25–20.

As the ball fell through the basket, an Ohio State player grabbed it, took it out of bounds, and threw it to one of his guards, who immediately took off down the court, hoping to catch Oregon off guard. But as Ohio State entered their offensive zone, they found Oregon already in place with their hands held high. Unable to pass to his forwards, the guard tried a long shot. John Dick rebounded and passed to Anet, who drove the length of the court to score. Following this spectacular play at just less than four minutes into the half, John Dick scored by tipping in one of Laddie Gale's missed shots, pushing Oregon's lead to 29–20.

Ohio state answered with a free throw by Hull and a tip-in by Sattler, but the taller Ducks continued to dominate the boards, and their speed and endurance began taking its toll on the Buckeyes. Anet made a free throw and Gale a tip-in before Ohio State's Sattler scored on a drive. With ten minutes left in the game, Gale took a pass in the key and one-handed it into the basket to put the Ducks ahead 34–25.

In the next five minutes for the Buckeyes, Schick tipped in a rebound and Lynch sank an outside shot; while for the Ducks, John Dick made two free throws, Bobby Anet scored on a drive, and Wally Johansen connected on a long shot to put the Ducks ahead by eleven, 40–29.

Growing desperate as time ran out, Ohio State faced an Oregon team that showed few signs of fatigue on either end of the court. The Ducks continued to dominate the boards and to run their fast break. In the last minutes, Wintermute, Dick, and Gale scored from the field and Johansen from the free throw line, while Ohio State managed just four points.

The final score: Oregon 46, Ohio State 33.

"Our big size advantage was a major factor in our success," said John Dick, who led all scorers with thirteen points, "as was the speed and quickness of our guards, which they couldn't match."

Another advantage was the coaching of Hobson. "In all my years," wrote George Pasero, "he was the number *one* basketball mind and innovator that I had ever known."

When NCAA officials presented the championship trophy to the Oregon team, it was in two pieces because during the game, while Bobby Anet was chasing a loose ball on the sidelines, he flew over the press table, and his arm knocked off the bronze basketball player standing atop the trophy. Anet landed in the laps of journalists, and the University of Oregon received a broken trophy.

But broken or not, the trophy was the first of its kind, awarded to the first NCAA basketball champion in collegiate sports history.

Celebrating after winning the NCAA championship (from left):
Wally Johansen, Bobby Anet, and Laddie Gale

The 1939 University of Oregon Ducks, America's first NCAA basketball champions.

Back row, from left: Bob Hardy, Red McNeeley, manager Jay Langston, Ford Mullen, Matt Pavalunas, trainer Bob Officer, Ted Sarpola, Earl Sandness.

Front row, from left: Wally Johansen, Slim Wintermute, Bobby Anet (with NCAA trophy), coach Howard Hobson, Laddie Gale (with Western Regional trophy), and John Dick.

The Aftermath

As soon as the people of Eugene heard of the Duck's victory, thousands turned out for a city-wide celebration. University students, townspeople, and other revelers crowded downtown streets so densely that city officials had to turn off the traffic lights. At the center of Willamette and Broadway, the Kappa Sigs set up a "Lemon and Green Victory Bell," and its peals of victory resonated throughout the town as blaring horns, exploding fire crackers, and crashing cymbals provided the background to a riotous pandemonium. The police were so outnumbered that they were eventually forced to join in the uproarious celebration that the *Oregon Daily Emerald* called "Bedlam."

Meanwhile, as they rode the train home from the championship game, the Ducks were unaware of the hysteria they had aroused in the Pacific Northwest—until they reached Oregon. Beginning at Nyssa on the eastern edge of the state, crowds began gathering at depots, waiting to get autographs, take pictures, or simply cheer the team.

As the train traveled west, the crowds grew larger, until it reached Portland, where 1,500 people waited to greet the new national champions. Oregon's

In Eugene, a crowd welcomes the new national champions.

largest city rolled out the red carpet, throwing a rally, hosting banquets, and holding a parade in honor of the team. Then it was on to Salem and Albany, where still more crowds waited, until at last the Ducks arrived home again in Eugene.

Waiting at Eugene's Southern Pacific depot was a throng of students, city officials, and townspeople who waited as the engine slowly pulled to a stop and the first player stepped down from the train. Then the crowd erupted in a roar of cheering and applause. The parade that followed was probably the largest ever held in Eugene, and the celebrations honoring the teams—ranging from banquets to dances—stretched into the following week.

"There has been no achievement in the history of the unified system," said Willard Marks, president of the State Board of Higher Education, "in which we have taken so much enjoyment."

Affection for the Ducks, however, went far beyond the university, for the entire region seemed to claim the team. After all, every player on the championship team hailed from the Northwest, and its five starters—Anet, Johansen, Wintermute, Gale, and Dick—were native-born Oregonians.

"The thing about those boys," Howard Hobson said, "is that they were truly an Oregon championship team. They were all born here."

But with four of those boys graduating soon, the magic they had created on the court would be leaving with them. And so it was time to say farewell.

"Goodbye, you Oregons," L.H. Gregory wrote in *The Oregonian*. "We'll never see you in action again in the Pacific Northwest...The color and the fire and galloping will not be there to the same degree...you belong to tradition now—the greatest tradition any Pacific Northwest basketball team ever left behind."

The architect of that tradition, Howard Hobson, agreed. "I think," Hobson said, "they were a group that comes along once in a lifetime."

Southern
KLAMATH
Pacific

Appendix

What Happened to the Tall Firs

Charles Robert Anet (1917–1980). After graduating from the University of Oregon in the spring of 1939, Bob lived in Lake Oswego and worked as a lumber broker. At the time of his death in 1980 at the age of sixty-three, survivors included his wife Paula and their two children, Peggy and Bob. "There is no question...Bobby was the greatest, most dynamic floor leader I've ever known," Howard Hobson said. "I've never known any driver like Bobby Anet. He really made that team go. His drive and leadership were the main cog that drove us to the national championship." The University of Oregon has retired Anet's number 20.

John Dick (born 1919). Dick served as student body president for the University of Oregon in 1939 and graduated a year later. After joining the U.S. Navy in 1940, Dick served throughout World War II. In 1946 he married Fran, his childhood sweetheart. He continued his naval career through the Korean War as well as in Vietnam, eventually attaining the rank of Rear Admiral. Now living in Eugene, Dick is an avid basketball fan and supporter of University of Oregon sports, and the "Rear Admiral John Dick Award" is awarded annually to the Ducks' best player. Fran Dick died in 1999. The University of Oregon has retired Dick's number 18.

Lauren Gale (1919–1996). In 1940 Gale graduated from the University of Oregon and married Hallie Marie Dudrey. Beginning in 1942 he served in the Army Air Corps at Long Beach, California, where he trained pilots in water survival and coached basketball. After leaving the service, Gale played semi-pro basketball. In 1950 he settled in Salem, where he owned a gas station for a short time, became a distributor of Master Bread, and worked as an automobile salesman. In 1964 he moved to Eugene and married Ginny Thompson, and two years later moved to Florence, Oregon, to sell real estate, a career that eventually took him and his wife to Gold Beach, where Laddie retired in 1980. In 1996 he died of natural causes at the age of seventy-nine. Surviving him were son Lauren Jr., and daughters Robin Terrett and Tia Menser. The University of Oregon has retired Gale's number 28.

Robert V. Hardy (born 1917). Shortly after his graduation from the University of Oregon in 1939, Hardy married his childhood sweetheart, Alicia. After spending two years in the service, he returned to his hometown of Ashland, where in 1945 he purchased his father's grocery store. After nine years of the grocery business, he invested in his first lumber mill in Happy Camp, California, and retired from the logging industry seventeen years later. He has two sons, Bob Jr. and William. Robert and Alicia now live in Brookings, Oregon.

Howard Hobson (1903–1991). Hobson coached at the University of Oregon until 1944, when he took war time leave to work with the U.S. Navy's V-12 program at Columbia University, and as a sports consultant for the U.S. Army. From 1945 to 1947 he resumed coaching at Oregon, but in 1947 took the

coaching job at Yale University while earning his doctorate from Columbia University. He led Yale to the Ivy league championship and a berth in the NCAA playoffs, the first in the school's history. Hobson later served as president for the National Athletic Basketball Coaches Association and as manager of the U.S. Olympic basketball team at the 1952 games in Helsinki. He wrote three books—*Scientific Basketball*, *Basketball Illustrated*, and *Shooting Ducks*—as well as numerous magazine articles. At the time of his death at age 87, Hobson was survived by his wife Jennie and their son. "He taught all of us to be winners, but we had to start with the basics," Laddie Gale said. "If there is a basketball court in heaven, I know who's coaching."

Wallace A. Johansen (1917–1971). After his graduation from Oregon in 1939, Johansen began law school at the university. His studies, however, were cut short when he had to return home to Astoria to help the family. There he became the sports editor of the *Evening Astoria-Budget* newspaper. In 1942 he entered the U.S. Navy and served as an officer in the Pacific. In 1944 he married Betty Grinde of Portland, then returned to law school at the University of Oregon, where he graduated in 1948. He and his wife then moved to Coos Bay, Oregon, where he became a partner in the law firm of McKeown, Newhouse, and Johansen. He served as president of the Oregon Bar Association in 1967-68, and was active in the Coos-Curry Bar Association as well as the American Bar Association. In 1971 at the age of fifty-four, while on a fishing trip with his family on the Rogue River, he died of a heart attack. Survivors included his wife, Betty; their two sons, Timothy and Kirk; and a sister, Beverly. The University of Oregon has retired Johansen's number 32.

Jay Langston (1915–1995). The manager of the 1939 team, Langston always considered his experiences with the championship team as one of the highlights of his life. He married in 1946 and later settled into a career in ranching and real estate in his hometown of Enterprise, Oregon. When he died in 1995 at the age of seventy-nine, survivors included his sons Nicholas and Jeffy and their families. His wife Billie preceded him in death, passing away in 1981.

Evert McNeeley (1916–1994). Following the Ducks' NCAA championship, McNeeley played basketball for two more years at the university before graduating in 1941. During World War II he served as a pilot in the U.S. Navy and was awarded the Distinguished Flying Cross. After the war he lived in Astoria for fifty years, working in insurance and real estate. When he died of congestive heart failure in 1994 at the age of seventy-eight, he was survived by a sister, Dorothy Turley, and his three sons, Jim, Scott, and Curt. His wife Jean had preceded him in death.

Ford Mullen (born 1917). After his graduation in 1940, Mullen married Jessie Steere. He played professional baseball until 1942, then taught and coached at Eugene High School for a year before joining the army. After his discharge in 1946, Ford returned to pro baseball before beginning a teaching career in 1950. For the next twenty-seven years he taught biology and zoology, and coached baseball and basketball. Ford and Jessie have three children—Judy Gayle Schneider, Jane Siemion, and Ford Mullen Jr.—and reside in Tumwater, Washington.

Robert O. Officer (1903–1972). The Ducks' trainer during their championship year, Officer spent twelve years at Oregon before joining the navy in 1942. After two years he returned to the university and, except for a four-year absence when he farmed, worked there until his retirement in 1968. "He was a teacher, counselor, father-confessor for all athletes," said Oregon's athletic director Norv Ritchie, "and a great part of the university's athletic family." At the time of his death in 1972, Officer was survived by his wife Elizabeth, daughter Nora, and son Robert.

Matt W. Pavalunas (1917–1991). After the 1939 season, Pavalunas played one more year for the Ducks, then served in the army during World War II. In 1944 he married Carolyn Taylor. After his discharge he finished his education at Utah State University, then taught and coached for twenty-five years at high schools in Washington. At the time of his death in 1991 at the age of seventy-four, Matt was survived by his wife Carolyn and a son Robert.

Earl Sandness (1919–1984). Following his graduation from Oregon in 1941, Sandness served in the U.S. Navy during World War II and the Korean War, eventually reaching the rank of Lieutenant Commander. Between the two wars he was a teacher and coach in Anchorage, Alaska. After the Korean War, Sandness taught and coached in Portland until 1979. He then moved to Ilwaco, Washington, where for two years he owned and operated a tourist charter boat. When he died of cancer in 1984, he was survived by his wife Dolores; his sons Earl Jr., Leif, James, and John; and his stepchildren Dennis, John, Paul, and Diane.

Theodore H. Sarpola (1916–1985). A sophomore during the championship run, Sarpola played another two years at Oregon. Following his graduation in 1942, he served for three years in the U.S. Coast Guard, where he also played basketball. From 1965 until 1981, Sarpola taught physical education, social studies, general sciences, and art, and sometimes coached basketball, at several Oregon secondary schools. At the time of his death in 1985, Sarpola was survived by his wife Dorothy and their five children.

John Warren (1904–1981). Warren coached at the University of Oregon for sixteen years, including five years as head coach, before resigning in 1951 to buy a Eugene hardware store. After Margaret, his wife of seventeen years and the mother of their daughters Susan and Corlene, died in 1946, Warren married Francis Elving in 1948. At the time of his death in 1981 at the age of seventy-six, he was survived by his wife, his daughter Susan, and his stepchildren Charles and Karen.

Urgel Wintermute (1917–1977). A graduate of the University of Oregon in 1939, Wintermute played professional basketball and later worked as a sales representative of Tolem Equipment Company, a general manager of the leasing division of Dresslar-Waesche Buick, Inc., and an analyst for Boeing in Seattle. On October 19, 1977, at the age of sixty, Wintermute disappeared from his boat on Lake Washington and was presumed drowned, though his body was never recovered. He was survived by his wife Carrie, two sons, and a daughter. The University of Oregon has retired Wintermute's number 22.

About the Author

After retiring from the Office of Public Safety at the University of Oregon in 1999, long-time Eugene resident Joe Blakely decided to concentrate his efforts on the writing of history. In 2003 those efforts were rewarded with the publication of the book *The Bellfountain Giant Killers* by Bear Creek Press, and the article "The Nestle Condensary in Bandon" by the *Oregon Historical Quarterly*.

Joe Blakey with fiancée Saundra Miles

"I had felt the passion of an era, the passion of people wanting a story to be told," Blakely says of his first book, *The Bellfountain Giant Killers*, and I made an effort to fulfill that wish."

Blakely also says that in *The Tall Firs* he found a basketball story every bit as passionate, but one that had never been told.

"There came to the University of Oregon in the 1930s," he says, "a pensive, detailed, progressive coach in Howard Hobson, and five basketball players who blended together so smoothly on the court that few college teams could stop them. Together they brought basketball to a new level of popularity that reached its zenith when they became the first national collegiate basketball champions."

Established in 1999, Bear Creek Press of Wallowa, Oregon, specializes in publishing books unique to the Pacific Northwest, especially those that capture the life or preserve the history of the region.

For more information or a free catalog:

Bear Creek Press

814 Couch Avenue • Wallowa, Oregon 97885

541-886-9020 • bearcreekpress@eoni.com

www.bearcreekpress.com

Bear Creek Press gives one-day service on all orders and an unconditional guarantee on every book.